WHAT'S COOKING IN CONGRESS?

Edited by

Harry Barba

Marian Barba

HARIAN CREATIVE PRESS

("One World Is Better Than None")

Adirondack-Metroland, Saratoga Springs, N.Y., 1979

First Printing, August, 1979

Printed in The United States of America

ISBN 0-911906-15-0
Library of Congress Number LC 79-83777

Mailing Address:
47 Hyde Blvd.
Ballston Spa, N.Y. 12020

Other Harian Creative Press books:
3 BY HARRY BARBA. Novellas
3 X 3: BARBA, BOND, HAMALIAN. Novella, Poems & Essay
HOW TO TEACH WRITING IN THE TIME IT TAKES. Monograph
THE SECRET CAREERS OF SAMUEL ROTH by Leo Hamalian. Bio-Essay
TEACHING IN YOUR OWN WRITE. Monograph
LOVE, IN THE PERSIAN WAY. By Harry Barba
THE THREE CRASHES AT MARSHALL UNIVERSITY ("Two Conn.
    Yankees Teaching in Appalachia"). Monograph
THE CASE FOR SOCIALLY FUNCTIONAL EDUCATION. Monograph
ONE OF A KIND - THE MANY FACES & VOICES OF AMERICA.
    By Harry Barba. Novellas & Short Stories

TABLE OF CONTENTS

PREFACE

CHIEF EXECUTIVE OFFICERS

MEMBERS OF CONGRESS

i

  * Ex officio
 ** Deceased

PREFACE

How does the idea for a cookbook begin? We can only speak for ourselves.

During boyhood and youth in a small New England industrial town, I peddled newspapers to help pay upcoming college expenses. Saturday afternoon, collection day, I rewarded my week's efforts by cooking myself a special snack. The ingredients were pork and beans, hot dogs, onions, tomatoes, and whatever other vegetables I found in the icebox. All of which I heaped onto one of my mother's pie plates and then shoved into the oven of our wood and coal burning Glenwood kitchen stove. Fifteen to twenty minutes later I sat down to what I called my "cowboy meal."

This was in the thirties and forties.

Ever since, the possibility of doing a cookbook or opening a special restaurant (or both) has been in my future.

But not until 1956 or thereabouts, and newly married, did the actual thought occur to me. A happy husband, mornings I took to frying, broiling, and benedicting eggs a certain way with all manners of fruit juices. Evenings, my turn at the stove in a household of shared responsibilities, I further experimented with fruit juices serving as the sauces for all kinds of shell fish and cooked vegetables. I spoke fantasies about spending my retirement as the proprietor of a restaurant called *Originals Only*. We would cater to a clientele with especially adventuresome palates. But that would be years off.

In 1970, mid-point in my career as an educator and fiction writer, I decided to devote at least one full year to completing a new novel. As a result, my wife took on the role of bread-winner and provider as a grade school teacher of art and humanities in a brand new open school system. In return, I took up some of the domestic tasks. After all, fair is only fair. So I found myself cooking most of the major meals during the week. Naturally I took up experimenting again. I strapped sauces heavily with fruit juices, fresh vegetables, and all kinds of fresh and canned fruits. In this way I made the most inexpensive but hearty cuts of meat palatable.

My wife enjoyed each new recipe as though partaking of a sheik's banquet of a thousand-and-one delights. She spoke of recording each new recipe in her diary. We looked forward to doing a recipe book of my creations in the near future.

Then 1973 — the Congressional investigations crescendoed in the public media and in the world's awareness. Like all Americans, I was affected deeply. I became absorbed in the daily television drama. Each evening I sifted out and pondered details from three or four newspapers. Weekends I pursued my search for understanding and judgment by devouring weekly and monthly magazines and the instant books that flooded the market.

One of the symptoms of my state of mind was that I lost interest in cooking.

The evening of the day the dignified and just Congressional inquiry finally led to the resignation of the man who was responsible for our nation's shame, I looked across the table to my wife.

"Congress cooks," I said through a mouthful of the trout she had not only broiled but had also purchased from the supermarket on her way home from a full day of grade school teaching.

"No, What's Cooking In Congress?"

"What?" Feeling my thoughts violated, I looked across the table. Her face smiling, I struggled to bring myself onto her wave length.

"The title of a recipe book — *What's Cooking In Congress?*"

Rising through my cloud of anxiety, I said brightly, "That's it! Let's do it."

And so, the beginning of this cookbook.

The next morning, I sat down and drafted the following letter:

Dear Senator or Representative:

Excuse this form letter in our attempts to reach as many of you as possible in the time set to go to press.

Do you have a special recipe you prepare yourself or your spouse or favorite chef prepares?

If so, we invite you to join your colleagues for inclusion in our cookbook now in preparation and titled WHAT'S COOKING IN CONGRESS? Favorite recipes might be one your mother prepared in your childhood, regional specials, or recipes especially fancied by your constituents.

You needn't worry about styling the wording of the recipe, unless you have a flair for such and pride yourself in that. We'll do the styling for you, with your permission.

The recipe will be designated as yours, and your party affiliation and the state you represent will be designated.

The purpose of our book of gastronomical pleasure? Just that — pleasure. And to show that Congress and Americans can still "cook" together and dine together even in the heat of and after a national campaign.

Yours for postprandial harmony,

Harry Barba, Executive Editor

P.S. This American smorgasbord of recipes will be edited by a husband and wife team.

The first week in January, 1976, we sent the letter out to each and every one of our U.S. Senators and Representatives. To ignite the kitchen stove, I followed the letter up with a few phone calls.

The results of our initial efforts were gratifying.

In many instances, responses were as formal as our letter of inquiry. We expected the majority of our solons were even busier than we were and so had anticipated this. But in greater numbers than we had hoped for, wives and mothers accompanied recipes with handwritten personal letters brimming with delightful tidbits of information about their spouses and sons. In some instances, the Congressmen themselves took the time to respond, and in their own handwriting. The latter tended to be as general and as affable as an afterdinner speech. A few did communicate on a personal level, ringing with warmth and sincerity. Isn't that what you would expect of our U.S. legislators?

We sent the form letter out a second time, after the elections — to freshman senators and representatives. We also wrote personal letters to President-elect Jimmy Carter and to Vice-President-elect Walter Mondale. In our letter to the President-elect, we suggested a full dinner menu from soup to nuts ("peanuts, if you wish," we wrote) might be in order. We diplomatically hinted we be spared another recipe for "Peanut Soup" since we had read several and various versions of these in the months of putting our project underway. Rosalynn Carter's assistant replied with the enclosed recipe which you will find in its appropriate spot heading up the main text of this cookbook. Joan Mondale's assistant also replied with a personal letter and a single recipe, not a full menu. These follow immediately after Rosalynn Carter's contribution. We expect the number of demands made upon the attention and time of our two leading ladies is reflected in their responses to our inquiries.

Needless to say, we are pleased with the cooperation we have received to our initial venture in what we expect will be a perennial gastronomical discourse between *we, of* and *for* the people of the United States of America, and the executive and legislative branches of our federal government. Who can say, maybe the scope of this book will someday include favorite recipes of the third branch of our federal government, the Supreme Court (should their august dignity not be put in jeopardy by so plebeian a participation). Why not?

As this edition now stands, our President and Vice-President and a quorum of Congress let it be known they dare venture into a real kitchen and face up to the real heat of a real kitchen stove. Seems like par for Capitol Hill appearances at roll-calls. Our hope is the second edition of this cookbook will be a unanimous attendance.

Before closing, we would like to share one of the problems we faced in making this book. Our project was conceived a full year and put underway nine months before national elections, '76. As a result, some of our correspondents had either retired or had not been returned to office by the time we began doing the actual book. What to do with their fine submissions? Following the logic *Once a Congressman, always a Congressman,* backed up by the realization that more than one of our legislators has been known to be returned to office after having been turned out to pasture, we thought of creating a special section titled "Ex-Officio Members of Congress." That is to say, *Those Not Cooking In Congress At Present.* Look at some of their names. Old friends, aren't they? So we decided to retain them, decorated and designated by an asterisk (*). We considered still another section titled, "Those No Longer Cooking Together In Congress." The latter, of course, would be made up of recipes submitted by husbands and wives no longer married or living together. We decided against this designation since the better part of politics is to be politic, especially in domestic matters.

As to the share of work that went into putting this initial book together, my wife and I discussed — even debated — the forepieces to each recipe. A couple of filibusters threatened but were headed off.

Arriving at a full consensus, my wife did the actual writing of the fore-pieces. The neatly devised indices were entirely her work. My tasks were mainly as initiator, organizer, and executive editor. Among the two or three friends who helped us with some of the chores, special mention should go to Karen Watson. A writer and artist in her own right, she did not find it beneath herself to do much of the typing of the first draft of the manuscript.

Conceiving, setting-up, discussing, organizing and putting this cookbook together has been a most salubrious and creative act for both my wife and me. Speaking for myself, the work has redirected my thoughts from the smoke of the more lugubrious ingredients of the Washington and national scene to the meat and potatoes of a more manageable (because more particular and everyday) recipe of interests, even if only temporarily. We have all been spending too much time (without relief) in what President Harry Truman spoke of as "the heat of the kitchen" of national and international politics. Perhaps we need to spend a little more time now in the heat of kitchens of less portentous and outsized dimensions. It is our finding that doing so helps us to feel, think, and work all the more comfortably in the "heat" of whatever our particular professional kitchen happens to be, politics, commerce, education, culture, or just-as-dignified (because just as necessary) common labor.

We have found this to be so. We trust you shall.

One last word and we have done for now. There were just the right number of "cooks" involved in preparing this literary "soup." We had some, but not many, near spoilings as the result of disagreed ladlings at the sauce of how to put the book together. Once we began cooking in harmony, the desserts of actually doing the book were a delight, full-up.

And so, WHAT'S COOKING IN CONGRESS? We've enjoyed our special kind of work in the "heat" of this special kitchen. We hope you find the results pleasing to your palate.

P.S. Because this project was put underway early in 1976 and for substantial and sufficient reasons was not published until 1979, the roster of those who wrote to us and submitted recipes becomes a household testimony to democracy in action. Of the seventy-six solons included, almost one third are desiganted ex officio, leaving us a working quorum. Who says our society and government is losing its most characteristic quality defined best by the word *mobility?*

We shall make every effort to see that our next edition is unanimous.

THE CHIEF
EXECUTIVE OFFICERS

PRESIDENT JIMMY CARTER

No, you-know-whats are *not* one of this recipe's ingredients. Instead there are pecans which, after all, start with the same two letters and are also a southern tradition. The First Lady's deputy press secretary, Ann M. Anderson assures us that this is one of the President's favorite dishes.

Plains Cheese Ring

1 pound sharp cheddar cheese
2 tbs. grated onion
2 tbs. milk
¼ tsp. pepper
Dash cayenne pepper
¼ cup mayonnaise
1½ cups pecan halves (about 6 ounces) grated in blender
   or finely chopped
Strawberry preserves

1. Shred cheese into a large mixing bowl. Stir in onion, milk, pepper, cayenne and mayonnaise with wooden spoon until well mixed. Stir in pecans until blended.

2. Pat mixture to a round on a serving plate, forming a slight rim around the edge. Refrigerate several hours until well chilled. Just before serving, fill center with strawberry preserves.

Makes about 12 servings.

VICE PRESIDENT WALTER F. MONDALE

On bright orange paper and illustrated with a pumpkin vine came Joan Mondale's recipe for Pumpkin Bread. From the Office of the Vice President comes word from Executive Assistant Bess Abell that it is the Vice President's favorite recipe. "It is a frequent visitor to the Mondale table."

Pumpkin Bread

Sift together:

1½ cups sugar

1 tsp. soda

¼ tsp. baking powder

¾ tsp. salt

½ tsp. cloves

½ tsp. nutmeg

½ tsp. cinnamon

1⅔ cups flour

Add and mix with beater:

2 eggs

½ cup oil

1 cup canned pumpkin

½ cup water

Add:

½ cup chopped nuts

½ cup chopped dates

Bake 1½ hours at 350 degrees

MEMBERS OF CONGRESS

REPRESENTATIVE JAMES ABDNOR, R.

It is not shuttle diplomacy that brings this Congressional memo from the Middle East to South Dakota to Washington and finally to us. Rather, it is one of Representative Abdnor's mother's recipes. She was a native of Lebanon.

Stuffed Cabbage Rolls

1 head of cabbage (two pounds)
1 pound of meat (may be lamb or beef that is ground or cut
    into ½-inch or smaller cubes)
1 cup of rice
½ teaspoon of cinnamon
½ teaspoon of salt
pepper
3 tablespoons of melted butter
1 Number 2 can of whole tomatoes
Juice of ½ lemon

Core the center of the cabbage and insert the whole head into boiling water to wilt the leaves. Drain and separate the leaves. Mix the meat and the rice (which has been soaked in cold water and drained). Add the cinnamon, salt, pepper and melted butter. Roll about one tablespoon of the meat and rice mixture in half a leaf of cabbage.

Line a saucepan with two or three leaves of cabbage. Add the cabbage rolls, arranging them evenly. Add the entire can of tomatoes and enough water to cover the rolls completely. Also add the juice of ½ of a lemon. Bring the ingredients to a boil and lower the heat to medium. Cook, covered, for about 45 minutes or until the rice is tender.

REPRESENTATIVE BELLA S. ABZUG, D.

The subtle art of understatement is not one for which political figures in general (or Bella Abzug in particular) are noted. To this, two "glorious" and "fabulous" recipes bear witness. And if the subtle art of patient waiting is not part of your cooking style, be sure to heed the final words of the cheese cake recipe.

Bella Abzug's Glorious Sweet and Sour Chuck

Boneless chuck — center cut and very lean
Sliced onions
One large can tomato juice
2 tbs. sugar

Put meat in a large pot, fill with onions, add 1 - 2 cups of water. Cook, covered, on top of the stove until the meat is tender and the onions have cooked down and are sticking to the meat. Uncover, add the sugar, and keep turning until the meat and sugar are one and a glaze has formed. Pour in 1 - 2 cups of tomato juice and cook uncovered until the sauce thickens and becomes brownish.

The main thing is: don't put much liquid in in the beginning or at the end. Add as needed as it cooks.

REPRESENTATIVE BELLA S. ABZUG, D.

Bella Abzug's Fabulous Cheese Cake

1½ lb. pot cheese
¼ lb. cream cheese
¼ lb. farmer cheese
6 eggs
1 tsp. vanilla
2 tbs. cornstarch
½ cup butter
1 cup sugar
½ cup sour cream
Graham cracker base

Strain the cheese twice through a colander — use the bottom of a glass. Add egg yolks, vanilla, cornstarch, butter, sour cream and sugar. Beat the egg whites until stiff. Carefully fold them in. Put in a spring form and bake in a slow oven (about 300 degrees) for 1 hour. Let it cool in the oven with the door closed. Don't look.

REPRESENTATIVE MARK ANDREWS, R.

Representative Andrews' recipe is part of a bulletin of the North Dakota State Wheat Commission. Although these rolls are promised to taste equally good in every state, we are told that it is the flour from North Dakota hard red spring wheat that is the real key to baking success.

Dakota Rolls

1 package active dry or 1 cake compressed yeast
¼ cup of water
1 cup milk, scalded
3 tbs. shortening
3 tbs. sugar
1 tsp. salt
1 well-beaten egg
3½ cups sifted enriched flour

Soften compressed yeast in lukewarm water (85 degrees) or the active dry yeast in warm water (110 degrees). Stir and let stand for five minutes. Combine the milk, shortening, sugar and salt; cool to lukewarm. Add the softened yeast and the egg. Gradually stir in the flour to form a soft dough. Beat vigorously. Cover with greased waxed paper and a towel, and let rise in a warm place (82 degrees) until double in bulk, about two hours. Turn the dough out on a flour dusted canvas or board and roll about ¼" thick in oblong shape about 8" x 16". Brush with melted butter and sprinkle with ¼ cup of brown sugar. Roll as for cinnamon rolls. Cut into 1" slices.

REPRESENTATIVE MARK ANDREWS, R.

Caramel Topping

Combine 1 cup of brown sugar, 2 Tbs. of light corn syrup, and 1 Tbs. of butter. Heat slowly in a greased shallow pan or in muffin tins. Set aside to cool. Place the rolls, cut side down, over the mixture. Cover, and let rise until double in bulk. Bake in a 375 degree oven for 25 minutes. Remove from the pan. Cool, bottom side up. This makes 2 dozen Dakota rolls.

California

REPRESENTATIVE ROBERT E. BADHAM, R.

Representative Badham sent a reprint of a *Los Angeles Times* article telling how he and his wife Anne enjoy cooking and planning special meals. Swiss Cheese Bread is a recipe that he has improved on after receiving it from a friend years ago. Could this be what really goes on in Congressional smoke-filled rooms?

Swiss Cheese Bread

1 cup milk
¼ cup butter
½ tsp. salt
¼ tsp. pepper
1 cup flour
4 eggs at room temperature
⅔ pound Swiss cheese, grated

Bring milk and butter to a boil in a 2-quart saucepan. Add salt and pepper. Remove from heat, add flour all at once. Stir with a wooden spoon until dough forms a ball. Stir in eggs one at a time until mixed. Don't beat or overstir. Stir in ⅔ of the grated Swiss cheese. Using ⅔ of the dough mixture, form a ring of 7 dollops barely touching on a well-greased baking sheet. Top each dollop with remaining dough. Sprinkle remaining grated Swiss cheese over all. Bake at 375 degrees until deep golden brown, about 45 minutes. Break apart and serve immediately with butter.

SENATOR HOWARD H. BAKER JR., R.

A double feature dessert pairs old fashioned home-made ice with new fangled cake-mix squares. Any relation to the American flag is purely coincidental, but, Senator Baker permitting, a topping of whipped cream and a maraschino cherry on the blueberry ice would please the patriotic eye as well as palate.

Blueberry Ice with Double Fudge Chocolate Squares

Ice

½ cup sugar
2 cups boiling water
2 tbs. unstrained lemon juice
1½ cups blueberry juice*

Cook the sugar with the boiling water for five minutes. Add the blueberry juice and the lemon juice. Then proceed with your ice cream freezer's direction for making ice cream.

*To make blueberry juice, press fresh berries through a sieve or through a potato ricer.

Double Fudge Squares

1 cup canned chocolate syrup
1 cup water
8 marshmallows (quartered)
½ cup walnuts or pecans
1 package chocolate cake mix

Preheat oven to 350 degrees. Combine syrup and water. Pour into 8" by 8" by 2" pan. Sprinkle marshmallows and nuts over the top. Beat cake mix as package directs. Pour half over syrup mixture. Bake 35 to 40 minutes. Serve warm, cut into squares, as is, or top with whipped cream or ice cream. (Remaining cake mix may be baked as cupcakes or layer for another dessert.) Serves 6.

REPRESENTATIVE DOUG BARNARD, D.

We requested a recipe. We received two of Representative Barnard's favorites, a bit of philosophy and the happy acquaintance of Mrs. Doug Barnard. With Nopi Barnard's permission we print one of her poems as well as her recipes. We were looking for a recipe. We found a cook, a writer, a poet — and a friend.

Georgia Pecan Pie

1 cup dark corn sirup (or cane syrup)
¾ cup granulated sugar
3 slightly beaten eggs
4 tbs. butter or margarine
1 tsp. vanilla
1½ cups pecans
2 uncooked 8 inch pie crusts

Boil corn sirup and sugar for about two minutes. Pour slowly over eggs, stirring vigorously as you pour. Add butter and vanilla. Pour, dividing equally, into two 8 inch uncooked pie crusts. Arrange half of pecans on each. The nuts will float. Bake at 350 degrees for about 30 minutes until pecans are lightly toasted and custard is firm. If desired this will make one 9 inch pie instead of two 8 inch. Reduce amount of pecans used to one cup. *Note:* Pecan pie to be really southern, should have sirup in it. When it is fully cooked the pecans will be lightly browned, but not burned, and the custard will be light and firm and luscious.

REPRESENTATIVE DOUG BARNARD, D.

Georgia Peach Pie

"Peaches," writes Nopi Barnard, "are another Georgia product and if you don't want to just eat them deliciously fresh with a little cream, try this peach pie."

> 4 cups fresh sliced peaches
> 1 cup sugar
> 4 tbs. all-purpose flour
> Dash of salt
> 1 cup cream
> 1 tsp. vanilla
> 1 unbaked 9 inch pie crust

Arrange sliced peaches in a pastry lined pie plate. Mix sugar, flour and dash of salt together and stir into mixture cream and vanilla flavoring. Pour over peaches and bake. If peaches are especially full of juice, reduce amount of cream used. This requires a 9 inch pie plate, 375 degree oven for 30 to 45 minutes.

*Mrs. V. M. Miller's Recipe For A Good Day

> 2 parts unselfishness
> 1 part patience
> Plenty of industry
> Kindness
> Smiles
> 1 loving heart

Work unselfishness and patience together; add plenty of industry, and lighten with good spirits and sweeten with kindness. Put in smiles as thick as raisins in plum pudding. Bake by the warmth which streams from a loving heart. If this fails to make a good day, the fault is not in the recipe, but in the cook.

*From *Company's Coming* cook book

REPRESENTATIVE DOUG BARNARD, D.

Dogwood in Autumn
By Nopi Barnard

Dogwoods shed red tears —
the season's passing
into a graying time
of evergreen and cold dark days.

Leaves do not pause
for human command,
nor robins for man's scheduled
hour to fly . . . .
through autumn's drifting, rustling days
I'm led
to say one more goodbye.

SENATOR DEWEY F. BARTLETT, R.

Whether the barbecue is in a suburban backyard or a pit dug in the midst of the wide open spaces, Senator Bartlett's sauce is sure to liven it up a bit. Where there's "liquid smoke" there's fire — barbecue fire, that is.

Oklahoma Barbecue Sauce for Beef or Chicken

1 tablespoon of salt
½ teaspoon of pepper
3 tablespoons of brown sugar
¼ cup of catsup
3 tablespoons of prepared mustard, or 1 tablespoon of
   dry mustard
2 tablespoons of Worcestershire sauce
1 teaspoon of liquid smoke (optional)
1 cup of water
2 tablespoons of chili sauce or 1 tablespoon of chili powder
¼ cup of chopped onion
1 clove of garlic, minced
1 cup of melted butter or cooking oil

Mix all of the ingredients together. When adding the oil, use a mixer to blend it better. Simmer until it is slightly thickened — 30 to 45 minutes. This will make 2 cups of sauce.

SENATOR BIRCH BAYH, D.

A quartet of recipes to be happily tabled comes from Senator Bayh with the Green Bean Casserole his personal favorite. Creative cooks might want to use the similar ingredients of the two casseroles with other vegetable bases.

Green Bean Casserole

2 packages frozen French style green beans
(or two cans No. 303 French style sliced green beans)
1 can mushroom soup
Grated cheese
Slivered almonds

If frozen beans are used cook beans until tender in ½ cup salted water, then drain. Butter a casserole, make two layers; first beans, then soup, then cheese, then beans, soup, cheese. Scatter sliced almonds over cheese topping. Bake 30 minutes in 350 degree oven. Serves six.

Broccoli Casserole

2 packages frozen chopped broccoli
1 can mushroom soup
1 stick garlic flavored cheese

Thaw broccoli slightly, salt to taste. Place in slightly greased casserole. Pour soup over the broccoli. Slice on top one stick cheese. Cook 35 minutes in 375 degree oven. Feeds four to six.

SENATOR BIRCH BAYH, D.

Fried Chicken

1 frying chicken cut into serving pieces
1 egg
1 cup milk
3 tbs. baking powder
1 tsp. Accent

Beat egg in the milk and dip chicken into milk and egg mixture. Roll in mixture of baking powder, Accent and flour. Add salt and pepper to taste. Pan fry. Drain on paper towel.

Oatmeal Cookies

3 cups quick oats
1 cup sugar
1 cup brown sugar
1 cup shortening
2 eggs
1 tsp. baking soda
1 cup chopped dates
1½ cups flour

Pour oats into shallow baking pan; place in 350 degree oven. Cream shortening, white and brown sugar. Beat in two eggs one at a time, add vanilla. Sift together flour and soda, dredge dates in flour mix. Mix flour mixture, warm oats and creamed mix by thirds. Start with flour mix. Return oats to oven to keep warm after each addition. Drop by tablespoon on greased cookie sheet. Bake twelve minutes. Remove from sheet immediately.

Maryland

SENATOR J. GLENN BEALL JR., R.

For those whose orientation leans more toward political science than to parapsychology, the similarity of Senator Beall's and Senator Ribicoff's favorite recipes might argue that when important issues are at stake, party differences are set aside. Or, perhaps, that great tastes like great minds work alike.

Apple Crisp

2½ cups sliced apples
½ cup water
1 tsp. cinnamon
A pinch of salt
1 cup flour
½ cup butter
¾ cup of brown sugar

Put the apples in the bottom of an 8" x 8" glass dish. Add water, salt and cinnamon. cream the butter, the brown sugar and the flour together. Cover evenly over the apples. Bake at 450 degrees for 10 minutes, then 350 degrees for 35 minutes. Serve with homemade whipped cream. This crisp serves 6 people.

Louisiana

REPRESENTATIVE JOHN BREAUX, D.

A Louisiana specialty comes to us from Lois (Mrs. John) Breaux. It is filled with savory seafood as well as enlightenment as to the nature of "file powder."

Environmental Gumbo

¾ cup vegetable oil
½ cup of flour
4 quarts of water
1 cup of chopped onions
½ cup chopped shallots or green onions
2 pounds of raw shrimp, shelled and deveined
1 pint of oysters
1 pint of fresh or frozen crabmeat
Salt and pepper to taste
Gumbo file powder (File powder is ground sassafrass; it
    is available in many specialty shops)
6 cups of cooked rice

Combine flour and oil in a large heavy skillet (iron is best). Cook over medium heat, stirring constantly. Do not let the mixture burn. Cook it until it is the color of chocolate. The roux can be made ahead and refrigerated. When the roux is the right color, stir in the onions; remove from the heat and set aside or refrigerate.

In a large kettle, heat the water; stir in the roux. Add the crab, parsley and shallots; bring the mixture to a boil. Cover, reduce the heat and simmer for about 45 minutes. Add the shrimp and continue simmering for 20 minutes. Then add the oysters and their liquid with salt and pepper to taste. Simmer 10 minutes and then allow to stand 10 to 15 minutes before serving. Spoon rice into soup bowl; ladle over the gumbo and sprinkle with file powder. Never add the file until serving; it will coagulate in the soup during cooking. Makes 8 to 10 servings.

SENATOR BILL BROCK, R.

The gentleman from Tennessee not only enjoys eating these dishes, cooking them is also one of his pleasures. A generous sampling of Senator Brock's favorites will suit a variety of tastes — something that Congressmen generally like to do.

Shrimp Bisque

1 pound frozen shrimp
¼ cup of butter
¼ cup of flour
1 quart milk
¼ cup of heavy cream
Salt and pepper to taste
2 tbs. Worcestershire sauce
¼ cup of sherry
Thin lemon slices
Paprika

Boil the shrimp; grind it up when it has cooled. Melt the butter and stir in the flour. Add the milk and cook, stirring constantly until thickened. Add the shrimp along with the cream, salt and pepper, Worcestershire and sherry. Put thin lemon slices into the warm soup. Sprinkle paprika on top of each serving.

Children's Favorite

2 fryers, cut up
1½ cup uncooked rice
1 large can of mushroom pieces with stems and juice
1 stick of butter (¼ pound)
1 medium onion, chopped
4 chicken bouillon cubes, dissolved in 3½ cups water
Salt and pepper.

Salt and pepper the chicken pieces, brown them in a skillet which has been liberally oiled and buttered. In a casserole, put the uncooked rice, chopped onion, canned mushrooms and their liquid. Put the browned chicken on top of this. Pour the bouillon over this, adding the butter in little pieces. Cover and bake at 350 degrees for an hour or longer. This holds very well, and will serve eight people.

Mint Sauce for Leg of Lamb

1 bunch of fresh mint
5 heaping tablespoons of sugar
Apple cider vinegar.

In the morning: Remove the leaves from a bunch of fresh mint which has been thoroughly cleaned. Chop up the leaves, and put them into a small, deep bowl. Add five heaping tablespoons of sugar. Cover this completely with apple cider vinegar, and then stir well. Cover and let stand all day long, stirring every hour. This is best if you grow your own mint!

SENATOR BILL BROCK, R.

Blender Hollandaise

½ pound of butter
4 egg yolks
2 tablespoons lemon juice
¼ teaspoon salt
Pinch of cayenne

Heat the butter to bubbling. Just before it is ready, warm the lemon juice and place it in the blender with yolks, salt and cayenne. Blend briefly, and immediately add hot butter in a slow, steady stream, while blending at a low speed. This will make 6 - 8 servings.

SENATOR EDWARD W. BROOKE, R.

Mothers of future Congressmen who are engaged in regular floor debate on the issue of eating vegetables will be heartened by Senator Brooke's recipe. As a matter of fact Caponato may well be the means for swaying negative opinion.

Caponato

4 potatoes
1 medium-sized eggplant
3 small zucchini
3 celery stalks
2 large onions (sliced)
½ pound cut fresh string beans
4 large tomatoes
4 green or red peppers
3 carrots

Cut the above vegetables into large pieces. Melt ½ pound margarine and ½ cup olive oil in a large pot. Add all the vegetables. Season with salt and pepper. Cover. Steam until tender. Serves 12.

REPRESENTATIVE JAMES T. BROYHILL, R.

How fitting a dish for a Congressman since in the orient *divan* is a council of state. Your Household Council for Domestic Affairs needs to schedule sauce-making a day in advance of serving and may vote Aye or Nay to the sherry flavoring.

Chicken Divan

4 pounds breasts of chicken
4 boxes of frozen broccoli spears
Parmesan cheese, bread crumbs
Sauce:
1½ cups medium white sauce
1½ cups undiluted cream of celery soup
1½ teaspoons Worcestershire sauce
½ teaspoon nutmeg
¾ cup mayonnaise
¾ cup whipping cream
Sherry (optional)

Cook the chicken in a small amount of water until tender, with slices of carrots, onion and celery added for flavoring. Cool, skin, and bone chicken, cut it into large chunks (do not dice). The sauce should be made a day in advance, if possible, by mixing the ingredients in the order given, except the whipping cream, which is whipped and folded in when the dish is prepared. Steam the broccoli only until it is tender, do not overcook.
(Casserole may be made several hours in advance and refrigerated.)
In an oblong casserole (approximately 13" x 8" x 2") place a layer of broccoli, over this a layer of chicken chunks, then spoon over half of the sauce, sprinkle with a generous amount of parmesan grated cheese. Repeat.

REPRESENTATIVE JAMES T. BROYHILL, R.

Finish with a thin layer of fine bread crumbs. Bake at 400 degrees until the casserole bubbles, and is hot through, about 15 to 20 minutes. This will serve 12 people.

If you desire a sherry flavoring, add 4½ tablespoons of sherry, or amount according to personal taste.

SENATOR ROBERT C. BYRD, D.

Senate Majority Leader Byrd sent us a booklet of his favorite recipes as prepared by his wife. Accompanying them is a family portrait picturing Senator and Mrs. Byrd, their daughters Mona and Marjorie, and a pet cocker spaniel, Billy Byrd. It is Billy who may just have a minority report to present to the Senator. His bone to pick is that although the main dishes are both beef, neither the Beef Stroganoff nor the Cabbage Rolls has a bone to pick! Thrifty cooks may find this more appealing than Billy does.

Beef Stroganoff

1½ lbs. round steak
¼ cup butter
1 cup sliced mushrooms or 1, 3 oz. can, drained
1 clove garlic, minced
½ cup chopped onion
1 can (1¼ cups) tomato soup
1 cup sour cream
Salt
Pepper

Cut beef into long thin strips. Brown well in ¼ cup butter in heavy skillet. Add mushrooms, chopped onion and garlic. Cook until lightly browned. Blend in tomato soup, sour cream, salt and pepper. Cover and simmer about one hour, or until beef is tender. Stir occasionally. Serve with hot cooked rice.

Cabbage Rolls

1 lb. lean ground beef
1 cup cooked rice
Small chopped onion
1 tsp. salt
¼ tsp. pepper
1 egg
Cabbage leaves
2 8 oz. cans tomato sauce
¼ cup water

Mix ground beef, cooked rice, chopped onion, salt, pepper and egg together. Trim off thickest part of stem from cabbage leaves. Divide meat into equal portions, wrap each in a leaf, fasten with wooden picks. Brown cabbage rolls slightly in Wesson oil. Add the two cans of tomato sauce and ¼ cup water. Cover, cook slowly about 40 minutes.

Pound Cake

1 cup pure white vegetable shortening
2 cups sugar
3 cups flour
4 eggs
1 cup buttermilk
½ tsp. baking powder
½ tsp. baking soda
1 tsp. vanilla or almond flavoring

Cream sugar and shortening. Sift dry ingredients together and add eggs, flavoring and half the milk. Beat two minutes and add remaining milk. Beat two more minutes. Bake in two greased waxed paper-lined 8 x 3 loaf pans in 325 degree oven for 45 to 50 minutes.

SENATOR ROBERT C. BYRD, D.

Lemon Meringue Pie

1 can (15 oz.) sweetened condensed milk
½ cup lemon juice
1 tsp. grated lemon rind or ¼ tsp. lemon extract
2 eggs separated
¼ tsp. cream of tartar
4 tbs. sugar

Combine lemon juice and grated lemon rind or lemon extract; gradually stir into condensed milk. Add egg yolks and stir until well blended. Pour into chilled crumb crust or cooled pastry shell. Add cream of tartar to egg whites; beat until almost stiff enough to hold a peak. Add sugar gradually, beating until stiff but not dry. Pile lightly on pie filling. Bake in slow oven (325 degrees) until lightly browned, about 15 minutes.

Graham Cracker Pie Crust

1¼ cups graham cracker crumbs
3 tbs. sugar
⅓-½ cup butter or margarine

Combine crumbs and sugar in medium-sized bowl. Stir in melted butter or margarine until thoroughly blended. Pack firmly into 8 inch pie pan. Chill one hour before filling, or bake in 350 degree oven for 8 minutes. Cool, chill and fill. Pie pan may be buttered. Remaining crumbs may be sprinkled over top of meringue before baking.

REPRESENTATIVE BEVERLY B. BYRON, D.

You might call the political careers of Maryland's Beverly and Goodloe Byron affirmative action in action. He preceded her in Congress for eight years. Whatever their respective voting records may be on affirmative action, the real vote will be cast in the future by who poaches the peaches and marinates the peas.

Poached Peaches

Boil & simmer
5 minutes

1 cup sugar
1 cup dry white wine

Add & simmer
to soft

4 pitted & quartered peaches
8 - 10 mint leaves pureed

Place in glass
bowl

6 peeled peaches

Cover with sauce and refrigerate overnight.

Marinated Peas

Mix

3 large cans lesseur peas
1 cup onions chopped fine
¾ cup green pepper chopped
¾ cup celery chopped
3 tbs. pimento chopped

Marinate in
and chill

½ cup sugar
½ cup olive oil
½ cup vinegar
½ tsp. paprika
1 tsp. salt & ½ tsp. pepper

REPRESENTATIVE BEVERLY B. BYRON, D.

Potato Leek Soup

Saute in butter
until soft

4 sliced leeks
1 large chopped onion

Cover generously with water or chicken stock
Add & Simmer
30 minutes

salt & pepper
4 large sliced potatoes

Add

½ pint sour cream & serve

Wheat Germ Bread

Mix & let
become frothy

¼ cup lukewarm water
¼ cup honey
1 tsp dry active yeast

Mix & let cool
to lukewarm

1¼ cup hot water
1 tbs. salt

Add to yeast mixture.

In Mixing bowl,
place

3 cups flour
¾ cup wheat germ

Add yeast mixture and beat.

Add

¼ cup olive oil

Beat hard in kneading motion 5 minutes. Put bowl in bowl of hot water and let rise. Beat down and place in oiled bread pan and let rise. Bake at 425 degrees 10 minutes and 350 degrees for 20 minutes. Cool and slice.

REPRESENTATIVE BEVERLY B. BYRON, D.

Meat Turnovers

Cook together	¾ lb. beef
20 minutes	½ lb. sausage
	2 chopped onions
	1 tsp. cumin
	½ tsp. coriander
	1 tbl. red wine
	3 tbl. chopped olives
Pastry	
Mix and add	2 cups flour
	⅓ cup butter
	⅓ cup Crisco
	1 tsp. salt
	5 tbs. ice water

Form into ball, chill. Roll into 5 inch rounds. Fill with meat mix. Fold and brush with egg. Bake 375 degrees 30 minutes.

Brownies

Melt over water	1 cup butter
	4 oz. bitter chocolate
Remove from heat.	
Add	2 cups sugar
	3 eggs beaten
	2 tsp. vanilla
	1¼ cup pecans or walnuts
Gradually add	1 cup flour

Bake at 350° for 40 - 45 minutes in 9 inch greased pan.

Iowa

SENATOR DICK CLARK, D.

Sure to win the approval of the Food and Drug Administration, Ralph Nader and American breakfasters is a recipe for home roasted granola. Senator Clark makes special note: "IMPORTANT: Make sure all ingredients are natural, with no preservatives or additives. The ingredients can be bought at natural food or health food stores."

Senator Clark's Favorite Granola

In a large roasting pan combine:
5 cups rolled oats
1 cup each of wheat germ, soy flour, powdered milk, sesame seeds, sunflower nuts, and chopped, mixed nuts.

In a separate utensil, mix 1 cup of honey and 1 cup of peanut oil. Add to the dry ingredients and mix thoroughly. Bake in a 350 degree oven for about 30 minutes, stirring two or three times during the baking to achieve the toastiness you prefer.

Store in air-tight containers. Serve with milk, or just plain. Granola is also excellent when eaten with yoghurt.

SENATOR ALAN CRANSTON, D.

With hope that others will enjoy the dish as much as he does Senator Cranston writes, "This one was handed down by my wife's Irish grandmother. It takes only five to ten minutes to prepare." It may take a few minutes longer to locate white cherries. Perhaps it would be permissable to use red cherries and tint White Salad a Washington cherry blossom pink.

White Salad

1 can white cherries (pitted) drain well
½ pound miniature marshmallows
½ pound blanched slivered almonds
Juice of ½ lemon
1 egg white
1 pint of whipping cream

Beat egg whites and the cream together. Toss in the other ingredients gently, and allow to chill in the refrigerator for at least a few hours.

SENATOR JOHN C. CULVER, D.

Political analysts have yet to consider the importance of the mother-in-law vote. If they ever do, our guess would be that Senator Culver has that bloc solidly behind him in the state of Iowa. The Senator sent us three recipes. One is, understandably, from his wife, Ann. One is from his mother, Mrs. William Culver. The third, as you have no doubt guessed by now, is from Senator Culver's mother-in-law, Mrs. Esther Cooper.

Sandbakkelse   by Ann Culver
(Sugar Cookies)

1 cup butter
1 cup granulated sugar
1 small egg unbeaten
½ tsp. almond extract
3 cups all-purpose flour

Cream butter, add sugar, and cream well. Add egg and extract.

Add flour to make stiff dough. Chill three hours or overnight. Allow to soften slightly before forming into tins. (Special Sandbakkelse tins can be purchased at a hardware store.) Take small ball of dough and press with thumb to the bottom and sides of tin evenly (must be 1/16 inch thickness). Place tins on cookie sheet. Bake at 375 degrees until golden brown or about 10 minutes. Remove from oven and tip the tin upside down and, as soon as they are cool enough to handle, pinch tin slightly to remove. They are very fragile. Sandbakkelse can be served with fresh fruit or whipped cream. Or my family thinks they're delicious just as they are!

SENATOR JOHN C. CULVER, D.

Orange Sherbet Salad by Mrs. William Culver

2 packages orange or lemon gelatin
2 cups hot water
1 pint orange sherbet
1 small can Mandarin oranges

Dissolve gelatin in hot water and while still hot, add the sherbet.

Drain oranges and add to gelatin. Refrigerate until set.

This is a quick, refreshing salad to have on hand!

Chicken and Macaroni Casserole
by Mrs. Esther Cooper

2 cups cubed cooked chicken
2 cups raw macaroni
1 can cream of chicken soup
1 can of mushroom soup
2 cups milk
1 small onion chopped
¼ pound shredded cheese

Pepper and salt to taste.

Mix all ingredients together the night before — let set overnight. Bake one hour at 350 degrees. Sprinkle buttered crushed corn flakes on top and return to oven for approximately 15 minutes or until nicely browned.

REPRESENTATIVE CHRISTOPHER J. DODD, D.

REPRESENTATIVE Dodd is a member of the House Judiciary Committee. Since three of his wife Susan's recipes have found equal favor in his eyes, he has judiciously submitted the trio.

Flemish Beer Stew

3 pounds beef chuck, cubed
6 - 8 slices of bacon
8 large onions, sliced
1 can of beer
1 cup consomme or beef stock
2 tbs. caraway seeds
1 tsp. thyme
Pepper

Brown the meat in bacon drippings, showering it with pepper. Set aside. Saute the sliced onions over a low heat until they are clear. Add the meat and the other ingredients. Bring the stew to a boil, and then simmer over a low heat for three hours. Serve the stew with rice or noodles.

REPRESENTATIVE CHRISTOPHER J. DODD, D.

Sherry Cake

One, 18½ oz. pk. yellow cake mix
One, 5½ oz. pk. vanilla instant pudding mix
4 eggs, well beaten
¾ cup of sherry
½ cup water
¼ cup vegetable oil
1 tsp. nutmeg
½ cup raisins (optional)

Blend all of the ingredients together in the order that they are listed. Beat well, until everything is light and bubbly. Pour into a greased 10-inch tube pan and bake at 375 degrees for 55 to 60 minutes.

Hot Curried Fruit Compote

One 1 pound can of peach halves, drained
One 1 pound can of pear halves, drained
One 1 pound can of apricot halves, drained
One 1 pound can of pineapple chunks, drained
One 1 pound can of dark and sweet cherries, also drained
2 tbs. of butter
¼ cup of brown sugar
1½ tsp. curry powder

Place all of the drained fruit, except the cherries, into a 2-quart casserole. Melt the butter in a small sauce pan. Add the brown sugar and the curry powder. Spoon this over the fruit, and bake for 15 minutes at 325 degrees. Carefully fold in the cherries, and bake for 15 minutes more. Serve warm as an accompaniment to meat. This will serve eight people.

SENATOR PETE V. DOMENICI, R.

This sauce's ingredients are rich enough for a meal in itself and bountiful enough to serve practically the entire Senate if no one has seconds. For smaller groups you may want to freeze a few batches and use as needed.

Mama's Special Spaghetti Sauce

6 lbs. good hamburger
3 lbs. ground pork
2 chopped onions
3 carrots
4 stalks celery
A little nutmeg
A little allspice
3 cans family size tomato paste
3 cans tomato sauce, large
3 cans tomatoes, large
1 tbs. sugar
4 to 6 quarts water
Salt and pepper

Brown hamburger and pork in oil. Add onions, carrots, celery, nutmeg, and allspice when the meat is browned. Add tomato paste and cook 10 minutes. Blend and add the remaining ingredients and simmer 3 to 4 hours.

(May add 2 large uncooked thighs and legs of chicken and when cooked, cut up, remove bones and put meat in sauce.)

Freezes well in plastic containers.

Virginia

REPRESENTATIVE THOMAS N. DOWNING, D.

Planning for the future is an element of sound government — and sound entertaining. Representative Downing's recipe can be mixed up ahead of time and, like an idea whose time has come, heated up for that special occasion.

Cheese Square Hors D'Oeuvre

8 oz. grated cheddar cheese
1 cup minced black olives
1 small onion, grated
½ teaspoon of curry powder
Mayonnaise

Mix the ingredients, adding only enough mayonnaise to bind the mixture. Remove crusts from thinly sliced white bread, spread with a layer of the cheese mixture, and cut the bread into squares, triangles or thirds. Arrange on a cookie sheet and bake in a 400 degree oven until the cheese melts and browns slightly. Approximately 5 to 8 minutes.

Missouri

SENATOR THOMAS F. EAGLETON, D.

There is no need for an interpreter when a twenty-four hour exchange of Sino-American influences takes place in the seclusion of your refrigerator. American steak and Japanese marinade emerge with a summit agreement sure to please all parties.

Steak Teriyaki

½ cup soy sauce
½ cup water
½ cup sugar
1 tbs. vinegar
½ tsp. garlic powder
1 tbs. ground ginger
Steak

Combine all ingredients in saucepan and bring to a boil. Cool. Pour over steak and marinate in refrigerator for at least 24 hours. Broil steak to desired doneness. Heat sauce to serve with steak at table.

REPRESENTATIVE EDWIN D. ESHLEMAN, R.

If the Messrs. Harris and Gallop were to poll Americans on their favorite desserts, pie would be sure to be one of the leading choices. From the heart of Pennsylvania Dutch country comes a pie with a regional twist. The liquid part is poured over the crust and when baked, ends up on the bottom — a phenomenon not unfamiliar to political pollsters.

Pennsylvania Dutch Montgomery Pie

Crust Part

2 cups sugar
½ cup shortening
1 cup thick sour milk
2 eggs
1 teaspoon baking soda
2½ cups sifted flour
3 unbaked pie shells

Liquid Part

1 cup sugar
2 tablespoons flour
1 pint boiling water
1 cup molasses
1 lemon (grated rind and juice)

Have prepared 3 unbaked pie shells. Set aside. Cream the sugar and shortening together. Add the eggs, one at a time, beating after each addition. Stir the soda into the sour milk, and add alternately with the sifted flour. Pour the batter evenly on the bottom of the prepared 3 pie crusts. To make the liquid, combine the sugar and the flour; gradually stir in the hot water. Add the molasses, and the juice and grated rind of the lemon. Pour this over the batter in the 3 crusts. Bake at 375 degrees until brown, and until the cake does not stick to an inserted toothpick. When the cake is done, the liquid part will be on the bottom.

REPRESENTATIVE HAMILTON FISH JR., R.

"This dish is bound to produce gastronomical and psychological tranquility, if not political peace," writes Billy (Mrs. Hamilton) Fish, Jr. in a handwritten note. The recipe is one that her husband is particularly fond of. As for tranquility of mind and stomach, folklore has it that rosemary averts the evil eye and restores the mind.

Rosemary Lamb Shanks

1 whole lamb shank per serving
2 or 3 small whole potatoes per serving
Salt and pepper
Minced garlic
Whole, dried rosemary

Preheat the oven to 275 degrees. Lay the lamb shanks side by side in a shallow baking dish. Rub salt and pepper and minced garlic into the surface of the shanks. Sprinkle liberally with rosemary. Surround the lamb with peeled potatoes. After the first half hour of baking, turn the potatoes to coat them with the juices that have collected in the pan. Continue baking for another hour, or until the meat and the potatoes are tender and brown.

SENATOR WENDELL H. FORD, D.

Senator Ford wishes all readers as much success with this recipe as his own family has had. It is "one of my long-time favorite cake recipes enjoyed since I was a boy." Who can argue with a seniority system that perpetuates such fare?

Fresh Apple Cake

2 cups sugar
1¼ cups Wesson oil
3 eggs
2 teaspoons vanilla
2½ cups sifted flour
1 teaspoon soda
½ teaspoon salt
1 teaspoon cinnamon
3 cups chopped apples
1 cup chopped dates
1 cup chopped pecans

Mix the sugar, oil, eggs and vanilla. Sift together the flour, salt and cinnamon. Blend the dry ingredients with the sugar mixture. Bake for 1½ hours in a greased and floured bunt pan at 300 degrees. Cool for 15 minutes in the pan before emptying. This cake will serve ten, and needs no icing.

Wyoming

SENATOR CLIFFORD P. HANSEN, R.

When Columbus sailed west in search of a short cut to India he happened on America by mistake. If his voyage took place today he would not be deprived of curry and rice — at least not if Senator and Mrs. Hansen were part of Washington's official welcoming committee.

Curry

1 cup of cooked veal or lamb
1 cup of stock
1 tablespoon of flour
1 small onion
2 stalks of celery, chopped
1½ teaspoons of curry powder
2 tablespoons of butter
1 handful of coconut
1 cup of cream of mushroom soup

Brown the onion and celery in butter. Blend in the flour and the curry powder. Add the cream and stock and blend thoroughly. When the mixture has become thickened, add the cubed meat and the coconut. Heat through and serve on steamed rice.

Steamed Rice

Place 2 cups of water in a saucepan and bring to a boil. Slowly add 1 cup of rice. Add one teaspoon of salt and one of butter or shortening. Reduce the heat as low as possible; steam for 20 to 25 minutes, tightly covered.

REPRESENTATIVE TOM HARKIN, D.

An Irish stew recipe, "one in which I utilize my personal cuisine skills," is Representative Harkin's choice. Membership on the Agriculture Committee and the Committee on Science and Technology may have enhanced those skills. Then again, it may just be the other way around, being at home at the range may have made him a better committeeman. The stew serves six — Irish or otherwise.

Irish Stew

4½ pounds of lamb neck chunks
2 tbs. butter or margarine
2½ cups water
2 tsp. salt
¼ tsp. each of pepper and thyme
3 medium potatoes
6 small white onions
1 package frozen green peas
¼ pound fresh or canned mushrooms, sliced
1 cup light cream or milk
¼ cup flour

Brown the lamb in butter. In a large dutch oven or kettle, add the water and seasonings, and browned lamb. Cover and simmer for 45 minutes. In the meantime, peel the potatoes and cut into medium size chunks. Skim the excess fat off the top of the stew after it has been simmering for forty-five minutes. Add the potatoes and the onions. Cover, and simmer for 15 minutes. Add the peas and the mushrooms, cover, and simmer for another 15 minutes, or until the lamb and the vegetables are tender. In a bowl, blend the cup of milk or cream with ¼ cup of flour, stirring and blending until they are well mixed and have no lumps. Pour this flour mixture into the stew, and boil for one minute, stirring constantly. Taste for seasoning and serve.

SENATOR VANCE HARTKE, D.

How, you may ask, did a recipe for real Italian spaghetti and meat balls find its way to an Indiana kitchen? Mrs. Hartke writes, "The following recipe for real Italian Spaghetti and Meat Balls was given to me by an Italian boy in New London, Connecticut in 1943. This is our favorite recipe and with seven children in the family, I find I usually triple the recipe."*

Spaghetti and Meat Balls

Sauce

Step 1 — Chop onion and clove of garlic in pan and fry in oil. Brown and add 1 can Italian tomato paste, empty in and stir with fork for 3 minutes and add 3 tomato paste cans of water, salt, pepper, ¼ cup sugar or more, 2 bay leaves. Simmer, season to taste and cook 1½ hours.

Meat Balls

Step 2 — In large bowl, put 1 lb. ground beef, 4 slices bread moistened thoroughly with water, 2 eggs, ½ cup grated cheese, ¼ cup parsley, 1 garlic clove chopped, salt, pepper and mix well. Dampen hands only to mix — no other water.

Roll in small balls and fry in frying pan. When brown on all sides, put meat balls in sauce for one hour or more. (I understand most Italian families simmer this for four to six hours.)

Spaghetti

Step 3 — Just before dinner hour, cook spaghetti until tender — allow ¾ lb. spaghetti per person.

SENATOR VANCE HARTKE, D.

Steps 1 and 2 may be prepared in the morning and then Step 3 later in the day.

*This does require 2 skillets, but after preparing this recipe a time or two, it can be quickly memorized — this hurries the procedure.

SENATOR WILLIAM D. HATHAWAY, D.

Small wonder that early New Englanders were so taken with Indian pudding. Corn and corn meal were unknown in Europe until introduced from the New World. Senator Hathaway and Connecticut's Senator Weicker represent two different parties but both favor Indian pudding. Perhaps their recipes come from different tribes.

Baked Indian Pudding

1 cup yellow granulated corn meal
½ cup black molasses
¼ cup granulated sugar
¼ cup butter or lard
¼ teaspoon salt
¼ teaspoon baking soda
2 eggs
1½ quarts of hot milk

Mix all of the ingredients thoroughly with one half (¾ quart) of the hot milk and bake in a very hot oven until it boils. Then, stir in the remaining half of the hot milk and bake in a low oven heat for five to seven hours. This is best baked in a stone crock, which has been well greased inside.

REPRESENTATIVE MARGARET M. HECKLER, R.

Dear to the hearts of all Congressional — and non-Congressional — cooks is getting a double return for a single expenditure of energy. Just that kind of energy policy is carried out in Representative Heckler's bake-one, freeze-one Shrimp Florentine.

Shrimp Florentine

4 packages (10 oz. each) of frozen, chopped spinach
3 pounds of shrimp
½ cup butter or margarine
½ cup flour
3 cups of milk
1 cup dry white wine
½ cup chopped scallions
2 cups (8 oz.) shredded cheddar cheese
Salt, pepper and paprika

Preheat the oven to 350 degrees. Line two nine-inch pie pans with heavy duty aluminum foil. Thaw and drain the spinach. Spread half of the spinach in each of the pie pans, top with the shrimp. In a saucepan, gradually melt the butter, stir in the flour, gradually add the milk, wine and scallions. Cook, stirring constantly over a low heat, until the sauce bubbles and thickens. Add salt and pepper to taste, and enough paprika for a rosy color. Pour the sauce over the shrimp and sprinkle with cheese. Bake one batch uncovered at 350 degrees for 35 minutes, or until bubbly.

Freeze the second batch. When it is frozen solid, lift from the pie pan and wrap in foil before returning it to the freezer. When ready to bake the Florentine, put it in a pie pan, pull off the top wrap, and bake uncovered at 350 degrees for one hour or until bubbly.

REPRESENTATIVE HAROLD C. HOLLENBECK, R.

A triumph of statesmanship combines two Mediterranean favorites to produce the hybrid, Moussagne. Lasagna and moussaka lovers will savor the best of both worlds. Representative Hollenbeck who wrote out the recipe by hand adds two words of advice based on personal experience.

"I personally favor my own-made sauce, liberally spiced and seasoned. It and the Romano provide a wonderful taste clash with the bland noodles and base cheeses.

A further key is to be sure to use a hot enough pan to make the eggplant crisp on the outside to seal in the eggplant texture and taste from the sauce."

Moussagne

¼ lb. lasagna noodles
Milk
Seasoned bread crumbs
1½ pts. spaghetti sauce (fresh preferred)
1 lb. chopped lamb or beef
2 tbs. olive oil
1 lb. ricotta
*1 lb. mozzarella (fresh) sliced very thin
*¼ lb. grated Romano (fresh)
2 medium eggplants
4 cloves garlic
2 eggs

*If available, I prefer a Greek cheese equivalent to the Italian cheeses.

REPRESENTATIVE HAROLD C. HOLLENBECK, R.

Saute lamb in olive oil, break up. Cook meat in sauce for fifteen to twenty minutes after adding crushed, uncooked garlic and pinch or two of sugar. Cook lasagna in salted water with one 1 tbs. of oil until al dente. Remove and quickly drain, cool, and return to pot with 1 cup warm water. Noodles are for top and bottom layers to bind dish together.

While cooking noodles, peel and slice eggplant about ¼ inch thick. Dip in bread crumbs, then in egg and milk mixture (¾ egg to ¼ milk), then in bread crumbs again. Brown until crispy in hot, lightly oiled pan.

Lightly spread sauce in bottom of square or rectangular baking dish. Place layer of lasagna noodles on bottom. I criss-cross them. Place layer of mozzarella over lasagna. Then alternate layers of eggplant, ricotta and mozzarella and sauce; eggplant, etc., occasionally sprinkling the grated Romano on the eggplant directly. The last layer will again be the noodles topped by the mozzarella and a light sauce layer. Bake covered at 375 degrees for 20 minutes; bake uncovered for 5 minutes.

SENATOR HUBERT HUMPHREY, D.

Popular with the entire Humphrey family, this was one of the valiant, late Senator's favorites. It has the added distinction of being, so far as we know, the only recipe in this collection that originated with a Senatorial father-in-law. Senator Muriel Humphrey noted, "This is a hearty old family recipe my father used to make . . . It's especially good for a light supper meal with fruit salad, a glass of milk, lots of crackers and dessert. It is low in calories, but high in food value. Serves 6 good hearty bowls."

Muriel Humphrey's Beef Soup

1½ lbs. stew beef or chuck and soup bone
1 tsp. salt
½ tsp. pepper
2 bay leaves
4 or 5 medium sized carrots, sliced
½ cup chopped onion
1 cup chopped celery
1 cup chopped cabbage
1 No. 2 can Italian style tomatoes
1 tbs. Worcestershire sauce
1 beef bouillon cube
Pinch of oregano or your preferred spice

Cover meat with cold water in heavy three quart kettle. Add salt, pepper and bay leaves. Bring to bubbly stage while preparing vegetables. Turn heat low and add celery, onions, carrots and cabbage. Simmer at least 2½ hours or until meat is very tender. Remove bone and bay leaves. Cut meat into bite-sized pieces. Add tomatoes, Worcestershire sauce and bouillon cube. Simmer for ½ hour longer and serve.

SENATOR HENRY M. JACKSON, D.

Though the Administration might not agree, the recipes in this collection seem to show Congress as assuming a positive role in foreign policy — at least in matters of a culinary nature. A good example is the Jackson family and one of their favorite desserts.

Norwegian Lace Cookies

⅔ cup of almonds
½ cup of butter
A dash of salt
½ cup of sugar
1 tbs. of flour
2 tbs. milk

Grind the almonds. Melt the butter in a skillet. Add the remaining ingredients, except the milk, and stir over the flame until the sugar melts. Add the almonds and milk, and blend. Drop from a teaspoon onto a greased and floured cookie sheet. Leave plenty of space between the cookies, as they spread flat while baking. Bake in a 350 degree oven for about six to eight minutes.

REPRESENTATIVE JOHN W. JENRETTE JR., D.

From the Office of the Majority Whip, ertswhile Freshman Whip Jenrette told us how to whip up a regional specialty. Prerequisites: one iron pot and one large hen.

Horry County Chicken Bogg

1 large hen
2 pounds smoke sausage
3 cups long grain rice
Salt and pepper to taste
Must cook in an iron pot.

Boil hen until almost tender. Add sausage. Skim off the heavy grease. Add three cups of rice to five cups of broth. Let simmer until it is done. Serves six.

California

REPRESENTATIVE HAROLD T. (BIZZ) JOHNSON, D.

Variety is the spice of life — and of a barbecue sauce. Straight from a member of the House Subcommittee on National Parks and Recreation comes a recipe whose very title starts the psyche unwinding.

Bizz Johnson's Mother Lode Chicken Barbecue Sauce

Combine the following ingredients:
2 cups of sauturne wine
1 cup of Mazola Oil
2 tablespoons of butter
2 medium chopped green onions
2 tablespoons of chopped parsley
½ teaspoon of thyme
½ teaspoon of marjoram
½ teaspoon of rosemary
2 cloves of garlic
1 teaspoon of salt
½ teaspoon of pepper
1 teaspoon of dry mustard
½ cup of ketchup
Dash of cayenne pepper
1 tablespoon of Worcestershire sauce

Bring all of these things to the boiling point, and then set aside to cool. Dip the chickens into the sauce at least two hours before serving time. Continue to cook the chicken, basting frequently with the sauce.

REPRESENTATIVE JAMES P. JOHNSON, R.

Rational consideration of alternatives is one of the classic steps in decision making. The choice of Representative Johnson's recipe was not arbitrary or capricious. "After several serious discussions with Mrs. Johnson, together we have decided that the following recipe is not only one of our favorites, but is representative of our home and the people of Colorado."

Chicken Enchilada Bake

1 large onion, which must be sauted in butter
2 cans (4 oz.) Ortega diced chiles
2 cans cream of chicken soup
1 can (13 oz.) Carnation evaporated milk
3 cans (5 oz.) Swanson's boned chicken
6 corn tortillas

Combine all of the ingredients in a skillet. Grease a casserole dish. Line the casserole with six corn tortillas, and pour half of the mixture into the casserole and top with grated cheese. Repeat layers. Bake for 45 minutes at 350 degrees. Or bake for 1 to 1½ hours at 300 degrees. Serves six to eight people.

SENATOR J. BENNETT JOHNSTON JR., D.

The bounty of garden and berry patch are main ingredients for recipes that Senator Johnston writes, "are two dishes that my family greatly enjoys." Since left over black-eyed peas are not a staple item in every refrigerator, directions for making them from scratch are considerably provided.

Black-Eyed Pea Soup

½ pound dried black-eyed peas — wash and pick through
the peas thoroughly
1 large onion, chopped
1 can tomatoes (1½ - 2 cups)
Ham hock or ham seasoning
Worcestershire sauce
Tobasco sauce
Salt and pepper

This is a good recipe for leftover black-eyed peas. But if you wish to start from scratch:

Soak the peas for two hours in water to cover. Bring to a boil. Add onions, salt and pepper, tomatoes, and ham hock. Cover and simmer for 1½ hours. Cook; mash through a sieve or put through a blender (meat and all). Add Worcestershire and Tobasco sauce to taste. Heat slowly, and if it is too thick you may add more water and seasoning to taste. This makes 6 servings, and is a good source of protein. It is nice to garnish this with chopped green onion.

Blackberry Pie

5 cups of blackberries
1½ cups of sugar
2 teaspoons of grated lemon rind
¼ teaspoon of salt
1 tablespoon of lemon juice
4 tablespoons of flour

Stir all of the ingredients together until the fruit is well coated. Pour into an unbaked 9" pie crust. Dot with one tablespoon of butter. Cover with a lattice-work crust. Bake at 450 degrees for ten minutes, then at 350 degrees for forty minutes, or until brown. Cool and serve with a scoop of vanilla ice cream on top.

REPRESENTATIVE ROBERT W. KASTEN JR., R.

Though Representative Kasten does not say so this recipe may date back to the day a certain cherry tree was cut down. In any event it would be a fine main dish to serve on February 22nd.

Chicken Montmorency

2 cups (about 1 pound) black pitted cherries
3 pounds of chicken
Salt and pepper
Paprika
3 tablespoons butter
1 tablespoon flour
1 teaspoon of sugar
1/8 teaspoon each of ground allspice and cinnamon
1 chicken bouillon cube
1 teaspoon red food color

Drain the cherries and save the juice. Wash and dry the chicken and sprinkle with salt, pepper and paprika. Brown the chicken on all sides in hot butter. Remove from the skillet. To the skillet add ¼ teaspoon salt, flour, sugar and spices; blend with the drippings. Gradually stir in the cherry juice. Add the chicken and the remaining ingredients, except the cherries. Cover, bring to a boil, and simmer for 40 minutes or until the chicken is tender. Add the cherries for the last five minutes of cooking time. Put the chicken on a serving platter and cover with the sauce. It may be served over rice.

SENATOR EDWARD M. KENNEDY, D.

Fish chowder is about as American a dish as one can find. The Pilgrims first landed on Cape Cod. It was fish and variations on that staple item that sustained them through the first year. If it weren't for the fish chowder simmering, there might never have been a turkey roasting later on. What an interesting opener this would be for a traditional Thanksgiving meal!

Cape Cod Fish Chowder

2 pounds haddock
2 ounces salt pork, diced or
    2 tablespoons shortening
2 onions sliced
4 large potatoes diced
1 cup chopped celery
1 bay leaf, crumbled
1 quart milk
2 tablespoons butter
1 teaspoon salt
Freshly ground black pepper

Simmer haddock in 2 cups of water for 15 minutes. Drain. Reserve broth. Remove fish from bones. Saute diced pork until crisp, remove and set aside. Saute onions in pork fat (or shortening) until golden brown. Add fish, potatoes, celery, bay leaf, salt and pepper. Pour fish broth, plus enough boiling water to make 3 cups liquid. Simmer for 30 minutes. Add milk and butter and simmer for 5 minutes.

REPRESENTATIVE MARTHA KEYS, D.

Not even the United States Congress has found the solution of how to have your cake and eat it, too. But Congresswoman Keys has figured out how to have your eggnog and eat it, too by way of this eggnog pie.

Eggnog Pie

1½ cups of milk
½ cup of sugar
2 tablespoons cornstarch
¼ teaspoon of salt
1 tablespoon of Knox gelatin
1 tablespoon of water
3 egg yolks
1 tablespoon of butter
1 teaspoon of vanilla
1 cup of whipping cream
Nutmeg

Scald the one cup of milk in a double boiler. Mix the sugar, cornstarch and salt with the remaining ½ cup of milk. Combine this with the hot milk. Add the egg yolks, gelatin (which has been dissolved in 1 table spoon of water) and butter. Allow the mixture to cool slightly, then add the vanilla. Fold in one cup of heavy cream, which has been whipped. Pour into the baked pie shell and sprinkle with nutmeg.

REPRESENTATIVE EDWARD I. KOCH, D.

The culinary specialty of New York City's mayor is a marinated hors d'oeuvre. Past and present concern with budgetary matters have perhaps influenced the uniquely expressed percentage rates of ingredients. One hopes that the Crazy Jane brand is not a must since outside of Washington and New York saner brand names — if not opinions — may prevail.

Raw White Turnip Hors D'Oeuvre

My specialty is an hors d'oeuvre and consists of the following: raw white turnips (the round type) sliced thin and marinated in a potion consisting of 60% olive oil, 40% wine vinegar and 200% raw garlic (meaning 2 large cloves) put through a garlic press, salted with Crazy Jane salt and Crazy Jane lemon pepper. Turnips should be kept in the refrigerator marinating for at least one hour, and served cold.

REPRESENTATIVE ROBERT KRUEGER, D.

A handwritten note accompanied by a recipe from Mrs. Faye Krueger, Representative Krueger's mother. "Bob Krueger is a bachelor. Also, he represents the 21st District of Texas which is the largest sheep and goat raising district in the United States. For that reason I consider this recipe most appropriate. Don't you?"

Butterflied Leg of Lamb

Debone a leg of lamb. Marinate it for several hours or overnight in the following marinade:

Lemon juice
Melted butter
Tarragon
Grated orange peel

Place on a griddle over low coals, fat side up. Broil it for 1¼ hours, basting both sides with marinade. The last 15 minutes, place pineapple slices on foil. Top with brown sugar and cinnamon. Broil over the coals. "Gutes essen!"

REPRESENTATIVE JIM LEACH, R.

Politics, goes the old saying, makes strange bedfellows. A coalition of apples and onions has been formed here that has the broad-based support of the Jim Leach family. They like it served with pork, chicken or other meat dishes.

Apple and Onion Casserole

3 large Bermuda onions
8 tart green cooking apples
½ cup water
Cinnamon, sugar, salt, pepper and butter

Slice Bermuda onions. Peel, core, and slice apples. Arrange in casserole alternating layers of apples and onions. Sprinkle apple layers with cinnamon and sugar and dot with butter. Sprinkle salt, pepper and butter over onion layers. Add ½ cup water. Bake at 350 degrees for 1 hour. Drizzle melted butter with cinnamon over casserole just before serving.

REPRESENTATIVE NORMAN F. LENT, R.

Noodle Pudding a la Lent is not a dessert amendment to the meal, but a part of the main bill of fare. The rules and regulations sent to us from Washington specify that the pudding can be served with a cold buffet or baked ham as a "vegetable-type accompaniment" but that it is *not* a dessert pudding.

Noodle Pudding A La Lent

Cook one 16 oz. package of broad egg noodles. Drain and rinse in cold water. Put in a large mixing bowl. Mix in one 16 oz. can of drained fruit cocktail, ½ pint cottage cheese, and then the following which has been mixed together:

> 4 beaten eggs
> ½ teaspoon salt
> 4 tablespoons sugar
> 2 teaspoons cinnamon

Pour this over the noodle mixture and mix well with 1/8 pound of melted butter. Put into a large loaf baking dish or a ring mold. Sprinkle one cup brown sugar, and about one tablespoon cinnamon over the top. Dot with butter and bake at 350 degrees for about 45 minutes.

Serve with a cold buffet or a baked ham dinner.

Maryland

REPRESENTATIVE CLARENCE D. LONG, D.

The greatest good for the greatest number is democracy's goal. This traditional baked bean recipe promises goodness to those who enjoy the leisure of eight hours for simmering as well as those who must economize on time via a pressure cooker.

Home Baked Beans

2 cups dried pea beans
¾ pound of lean salt pork
5 tablespoons of dark brown sugar
2 tablespoons of molasses
1 teaspoon of dried English mustard
Boiling water

Pick over the beans and throw out any dark gray or black ones. Put them in a strainer and wash under cold running water. Put into a bowl and cover with cold water. Soak the beans overnight. Drain, cover with fresh water, and heat slowly (keeping water below the boiling point) until the skins burst open if a few beans are held on the end of a spoon and blown upon.

Scald the pork by frying it briefly on all six sides. Cut through the rind of pork every half inch with one-inch deep cuts. Put the pork in a pot, and cover with the drained beans. Boil about 2 cups of water, and dissolve the sugar and molasses in it. Add a teaspoon of mustard to a teaspoon of cold water, and stir into a paste. Add the mustard paste to the liquid mixture and stir. Add the liquid mixture to the beans and pork. Add enough extra boiling water to cover the beans. Cover the bean pot and bake at 250 degrees for about eight hours. Check every two hours to make sure that the beans are covered with water.

REPRESENTATIVE CLARENCE D. LONG, D.

Cooking time of the beans may be greatly shortened by using a pressure cooker. Set the control of the pressure cooker at 15, and cook at least 25 minutes after the control jiggles. Reduce the pressure normally. Taste to see if the beans are of desired softness. If not, return them to the stove and cook under pressure for 15 minutes, after making certain that the beans are covered with boiling water.

SENATOR RICHARD G. LUGAR, R.

Indiana's history dates back to the days of the Northwest Territory. The chipped beef in one of these Lugar family favorites would have been quite familiar to the state's earliest Congressional delegates but the mushroom soup is strictly twentiety century.

Chicken-Beef Supreme

6 deboned chicken breasts — split
1 package dried chipped beef
1 can cream of mushroom soup
1 cup sour cream

Lightly grease a pyrex dish, line with slices of chipped beef. Place chicken breasts over beef. Mix soup and sour cream together and spread over the chicken breasts. Sprinkle with Romano or Parmesan cheese. Bake at 250 degrees for 2 hours. (May be prepared the day before and refrigerated until time to bake.)

Rice Casserole

2 cans mushrooms and liquid (small can)
2 cups Uncle Ben's unconverted rice
2 sticks margarine
1½ tsp. oregano
2 cans beef consomme
2 cans water

Mix together and bake at 350 degrees for one hour. This is a side dish.

SENATOR GEORGE McGOVERN, D.

The fourth Friday in November may be as significant to leftover turkey users as the second Tuesday in November is to would-be Congressmen. Mrs. McGovern's casserole recipe gives two choices for the main ingredient making it a fine dish to prepare on either day.

Chicken (Or Turkey) Casserole

- 2 packages of frozen, chopped broccoli (defrosted and thoroughly drained)
- 2 cans of celery soup
- 2 cups of cooked chicken or turkey
- 1 can of sliced water chestnuts
- 1 large can of mushrooms, buttered and broiled

Mix all of these ingredients together, and place in a casserole, with shredded almonds over the top. Bake for 1 hour in a 350 degree oven. This will serve 6 to 8 people.

REPRESENTATIVE GUNN McKAY, D.

Webster's New World Dictionary defines rhubarb as American slang for a heated discussion or argument. No such rhubarb is likely to occur in Congress or elsewhere over the gastronomical merits of Mrs. McKay's cobbler.

Rhubarb Cobbler

3 cups of diced rhubarb
2 table spoons of butter
1 cup of sugar
Blend these ingredients and put into a 350 degree oven,
    while preparing the rest of the recipe.
1½ cups of flour
¼ teaspoon of salt
3 teaspoons of baking powder
¾ cup of shortening
1 beaten egg
½ cup of milk

Cut the shortening into the dry ingredients. Add the egg and the milk. Pour this over the other mixture, and bake for 30 to 45 minutes in a 350 degree oven.

REPRESENTATIVE LLOYD MEEDS, D.

Is there, perhaps, somewhere in Outer Mongolia a government official who proudly serves his dinner guests a dish called American Beef? We can not be sure of that. What we can be sure of is that Mongolian Beef is Representative Meeds' favorite recipe and that he is willing to share it.

Mongolian Beef

1½ pounds of sirloin steak, or round steak thinly sliced
   (1/16 of an inch thick)
2 small cloves of garlic
½ cup of sauterne
½ cup of oyster sauce
1 tablespoon of cornstarch
½ teaspoon of sugar
½ teaspoon of salt
2 tablespoons of peanut oil
5 heads of large spring onions, sliced lengthwise (1/8")
½ cup of fresh snow peas, or ½ package of frozen snow
   peas, thawed and thoroughly drained

Marinate the beef in the sauterne, oyster sauce, sugar and salt, garlic and cornstarch. Use your hands to mix well. Place in the refrigerator for two hours. Heat the oil in a frying pan over a high heat. Add the beef and stir constantly until brown. Add the onion, snow peas and ½ cup of water. Continue stirring for 2 to 3 minutes and serve. This is enough for 6 to 8 people.

REPRESENTATIVE PATSY T. MINK, D.

Involvement with Insular Affairs is decided pleasure when said affairs include Spareribs Hawaiian. Able cooks — like able Congressmen — will reach a compromise if necessary on the issue of fresh papaya. It is the only ingredient not readily available throughout the country.

Spareribs Hawaiian

2 pounds of lean spare ribs
3 tbs. flour
1 tsp. salt
3 tbs. soy sauce
3 tbs. salad oil
⅔ cups sugar
⅔ cups wine vinegar
½ cup water
½ cup pineapple juice
1 tsp. grated fresh ginger root or ½ tsp. dry ginger
2 cups fresh pineapple and papaya chunks

Cut the spare ribs into 2 inch pieces. Mix the flour, salt and soy sauce together, and coat the ribs. Allow to stand for 10 minutes. Heat the oil in a skillet and brown the ribs on all sides. Drain off the excess fat, and add sugar, vinegar, water, juice and ginger. cover, simmer until the meat is tender, about 45 minutes. stir in the fruit and simmer for 5 minutes longer. Serve garnished with minced parsley and sesame seeds.

REPRESENTATIVE DONALD J. MITCHELL, R.

A cheese ball that has been "a Mitchell family favorite for may years" is a likely recipe to come from the native son of a dairy — and wine — producing state. Since no particular party is specified in the name we assume it's appropriate to serve at, and to, all parties.

Party Cheese Ball

1 package (8 oz.) cream cheese
¾ cup crumbled blue cheese (about 4 oz.)
1 cup shredded blue cheese (about 4 oz.)
¼ cup minced onion
1 tablespoon Worcestershire sauce
Finely snipped parsley

Place the cheeses in a small mixer bowl; let stand at room temperature until softened. Add onion and Worcestershire sauce; blend on low speed. (If a blender is not available, creaming and then beating by hand works well. There were cheese balls before there were electric mixers.) Then, beat on medium speed until fluffy, scraping the sides and the bottom of the bowl. Cover; chill at least eight hours.

Shape the mixture into one large ball or 30-36 one-inch balls. Roll in parsley; place on a serving plate. Cover; chill two hours or until firm. For variety, the ball may be rolled in chopped nuts instead of parsley.

REPRESENTATIVE AUSTIN J. MURPHY, D.

A recipe that would have been downright illegal during Prohibition is edible proof that the 18th Amendment was repealed by the 21st. Representative Murphy serves on the Labor and Interior Committees. His Frozen Daiquiris are easy on both.

Frozen Banana Daiquiris

2 bananas
1 pint vanilla or coconut ice cream
1 tsp. shredded coconut
4 oz. rum

Mash up bananas and combine with shredded coconut and ice cream. Mix together and add rum. Spoon mixture into parfait glasses. Place in freezer and serve in two to three hours.

SENATOR EDMUND S. MUSKIE, D.

"**O**ur big family likes simple, hearty meals," writes Jane Muskie. "Particularly this recipe which always seems to turn the table conversations at our house to thoughts of Maine. I like to serve a New England dinner for practical reasons, too. It means freedom from the kitchen in the afternoon and few last minute details at night. I usually serve this boiled beef dinner with horseradish, mustard pickle and hot buttered bread. (I save the broth for soup.) My husband and children like fresh fruit and brownies to top it off."

Jane Muskie's New England Dinner

4 - 5 pound corned brisket of beef
Cold water to cover
½ bay leaf
5 whole peppercorns
Basil, thyme, parsley
6 white or yellow turnips, peeled and sliced
8 whole carrots, scraped
4 parsnips (peeled) if you like
10 small onions, peeled
8 medium potatoes, peeled
1 green cabbage, cored and cut into wedges

Place the beef in a deep kettle and cover with cold water, adding the spices, but NO salt. Bring water to a boil. Skim off the fat. Then cover and simmer for 3 - 4 hours. Add all the vegetables but the cabbage and continue to cook about 20 minutes. Add cabbage and cook until all vegetables are tender (about 25 minutes longer). Place beef on a very hot platter, surround with the vegetables.

REPRESENTATIVE WILLIAM H. NATCHER, D.

Corn and peach pudding are both "long-time and great favorites in our family," writes Congressman Natcher. Since the proof of the pudding is in the eating there's a pleasant way to prove his point.

Corn Pudding

2 tablespoons butter or margarine
2 tablespoons salad oil
½ onion, chopped fine
1 cup whole kernel corn (canned or fresh)
1 tablespoon sugar
Salt and pepper to taste
3 eggs, separated
½ cup cheddar cheese, grated or chopped fine

Heat the butter and salad oil in a skillet. Saute onion, and add the corn, sugar, salt and pepper. Cool slightly and add the cheese and the well-beaten egg yolks. Fold in the stiffly beaten egg whites. Pour in a well greased 9 x 11 inch casserole and set in a pan of hot water. Bake in a 350 degree oven for one hour. Serve the pudding at once to four people.

REPRESENTATIVE WILLIAM H. NATCHER, D.

Baked Peach Pudding

1 cup flour
⅔ cup flour
⅔ cup sweet milk
1 teaspoon baking powder
1 teaspoon salt
½ cup melted butter
2 cups sliced peaches (or any other fruit)

Place the peaches in a pan and bring to a boiling point with the peach syrup as the liquid. Add a little sugar if the syrup is not thick. Combine the other ingredients to make a batter, and pour this over the peaches. Bake in a 325 degree oven for about 45 minutes, or until the baked pudding is done.

SENATOR GAYLORD NELSON, D.

East is east and west is west. Sometimes the twain do meet outside of the State Department. In Senator Nelson's kitchen, for example, where oriental dumplings meet with occidental approval.

Gaylord Nelson's Jao-Tze

1 pound lean ground beef
2 tablespoons soy sauce
2 tablespoons dry sherry
1 small green pepper, chopped
1½ large onions, chopped
½ stalk celery, diced
4 waterchestnuts, diced
Salt, to taste

Brown the beef and pour off the fat. Stir in the soy sauce and the sherry, and simmer for a moment or two. Add the vegetables and cook for a few minutes. The vegetables should still be crisp. Season with salt, if necessary. Pour the mixture into a strainer, and allow to cool and drain while making the dough. Use this as a filling for Jao-tze dough.

SENATOR GAYLORD NELSON, D.

Hot Water Dough

3 cups of flour
About one cup of hot water.

As you pour the water into the flour, stir with a fork, until it gathers into sticky balls. Use your hands to gather all of the dough into one ball, and then knead for about five minutes until the dough is smooth. If necessary, use more flour in kneading. Shape the dough into a smooth ball and set on a plate. Cover it to keep the dough from drying out. Break off pieces that are a little larger than the size of a golf ball. Flatten the dough with your hands, and roll out on a floured surface to circles, turning and flouring the dough as you must. The circle must be large enough to cut from it a perfect circle between 7½ and 8 inches. Fill this circle with a scant ½ cup filling and fold the dough over, like a half moon. Then press the edges together, pleating them at the same time, so that the edges look ruffled when you are finished. Flatten slightly and cover until several dumplings are ready to be cooked. Either saute in a little hot oil on both sides and on the bottom until golden brown, or steam the dumplings over hot water for 20 minutes. Serve with a mixture of equal parts of soy sauce and vinegar, which can be poured into the dumpling after the first bite is taken. The dumplings can also be made quite small, by cutting into 4 inch circles. The same directions would apply, except they should be filled with 2 teaspoons of filling. This recipe makes 10 large dumplings or 25 small ones.

Rhode Island

SENATOR JOHN O. PASTORE, D.

Whether your dinner table constituency supports gourmet cooking or basic meat and potatoes, Mrs. Pastore's braciola recipe will tie up their vote along with the round steaks.

Meat Roll (Braciola) Stew

4 thinly sliced bottom round steaks
½ teaspoon salt, ¼ teaspoon pepper
1/8 teaspoon garlic salt
½ cup bread crumbs
1 tablespoon grated cheese
1 teaspoon chopped parsley
4 peeled whole potatoes
4 peeled whole onions
4 pared whole carrots
1 cut-up stalk of celery
2 tablespoons oil or margarine
1 cup of water

Mix together in a bowl, salt, pepper, garlic salt, bread crumbs, grated cheese and parsley. Spread this mixture onto four slices of meat. Roll into four rolls (or braciola) and tie with string.

Brown in deep pan in oil or margarine, turning to brown on all sides.

If desired, add 2 tablespoons of wine. Add water. Add all of the peeled and washed vegetables, and lay on top of the meat. Do not turn the vegetables. Add more salt and pepper to taste if desired. Cover the pan, and cook slowly for one hour or until the potatoes are tender. Remove the string before serving. This will serve four.

REPRESENTATIVE EDWARD J. PATTEN, D.

Representative Patten probably just likes green beans but it is a politically happy coincidence for a representative of the Garden State. (Not too surprisingly, chicken a la king does *not* appear in this volume of Congressional favorites.)

Green Bean Casserole

One 10 oz. can of mushroom soup
½ cup light cream or milk
1 tbs. flour
1 tbs. butter
½ tsp. Worcestershire
½ cup grated cheddar cheese
4 cups cooked string beans
2 tbs. chopped pimento
Salt and pepper to taste
½ cup buttered bread crumbs
⅓ cup Parmesan cheese

Combine the soup and the cream, and heat. Blend the flour and the butter; stir it into the soup. Add the Worcestershire, and stirring constantly, cook until thick. Stir the cheese in until it is melted. Combine this mixture with the beans and the pimento, and season to taste. Pour into a casserole dish, sprinkle with the bread crumbs and Parmesan cheese. Bake at 350 degrees for 20 minutes. This will serve 6 - 8 people.

REPRESENTATIVE EDWARD W. PATTISON, D.

Two favorite recipes from the Edward W. Pattison family show that within the House (or the house) there is room for dissent. As for the Representative's taste for grits, Congress must be a place where a true exchange of ideas does take place. His 29th Congressional District is not even in the southern part of New York.

Congressman Ned Pattison's Favorite:

Grits and Sausage Breakfast

Prepare hominy grits per instructions on package (use more water than called for to avoid excessive stiffness). Prepare link or patty sausage, fry at high temperature at beginning to achieve good browning. Prepare gravy from sausage brownings and about a tablespoon of sausage drippings. Serve grits in bowl with sausage on top; add gravy, salt and butter to taste.

REPRESENTATIVE EDWARD W. PATTISON, D.

Ellie Pattison's, Congressman Pattison's Wife's, Favorite:

Green Beans A La Ellie Pattison

3 packages frozen green beans (French)

Sauce

2 tbs. butter
2 tbs. flour
1 tbs. salt
2 tbs. sugar
Small package Swiss cheese
1 tbs. chopped onion

Partially cook beans as directed on package, drain. Combine all sauce ingredients in sauce pan over moderate heat until smooth and creamy. Pour over beans arranged in oven-proof casserole. Sprinkle with bread crumbs. Serve immediately or make ahead, freeze and reheat in oven at 350 degrees.

SENATOR ABRAHAM R. RIBICOFF, D.

One of Lois (Mrs. Abraham) Ribicoff's favorite recipes is Deep Apple Pot-Pie which she graciously sent to share with us. At about the same time then Senator J. Glenn Beall sent us a recipe for his favorite Apple Crisp. On reading the two we were struck by their similarity. We note the coincidence with the thought that ESP seems alive, well and thriving in Washington. After all, both Ruth Montgomery and Jeanne Dixon call it home.

Deep Apple Pot-Pie

6 firm, medium baking apples
Cinnamon
Sugar
Butter
½ pint whipping cream
A pinch of salt
Lemon juice
Maple or light brown sugar
Walnuts or pecan halves.

Pare, core and slice the apples. Place the apple slices in a buttered baking dish, and sprinkle each layer generously with cinnamon and sugar. Dot each layer generously with butter. Continue layering the apples until the dish is nearly full.

SENATOR ABRAHAM R. RIBICOFF, D.

Then prepare:

Crumbly Mixture For The Top

½ cup butter
1 cup of brown sugar
¾ cup flour
1 tsp. of cinnamon
½ teaspoon of salt

Combine all the ingredients into Crumbly Mixture. Sprinkle thickly over the apples. Bake in 350 degree oven until the apples are tender, and the topping is crusty and glazed. Serve hot or cold with freshly whipped cream with nuts sprinkled on top.

REPRESENTATIVE FRED B. ROONEY, D.

Legend has it that Benjamin Franklin walked into Philadelphia with a couple of rolls tucked under his arm which makes baked goods practically a part of Pennsylvania history. A cake recipe, then from the home of Betsy Ross, Congressman Rooney and Hershey chocolate.

Pennsylvania Sheet Cake

Cake

2 sticks of butter or margarine
1 cup of water
4 tbs. cocoa
2 cups of all purpose flour
2 cups of sugar
½ tsp. salt
2 eggs
½ cup of sour cream
1 tsp. baking soda

In a saucepan mix the butter, water and cocoa, and bring to a boil. In a large bowl, combine the flour, sugar and salt; add the hot liquid to this and heat well. Add the eggs, sour cream and soda, beating the mixture well. Pour everything into a greased and floured pan. Bake in a preheated 350 degree oven for twenty to thirty minutes.

REPRESENTATIVE FRED B. ROONEY, D.

Icing

1 stick butter or margarine
4 tbs. cocoa
4 tbs. milk
1 pound of confectioner's sugar

Mix the butter, the cocoa and milk in a saucepan. Bring to a boil, and remove from the heat. Add the confectioner's sugar and milk alternately, beating well after each addition. Ice the cake as soon as it is taken out of the oven. Add nuts on top of the cake for a finishing touch.

SENATOR JIM SASSER, D.

Would that arms talks and human rights were as easy to agree upon as international cuisine. A handwritten recipe card from Rary (Mrs. Jim) Sasser is a case in point. No negotiations needed, just a hearty appetite.

Beef Stroganoff

2 pounds beef tenderloin cut in strips
1 tbs. flour
2 tbs. butter
2 cups beef stock
1 pound fresh mushrooms
4 tbs. sour cream
4 tbs. tomato paste
1 large onion grated

Sprinkle beef with salt and pepper. Blend flour and butter over low heat, add beef stock, cook until it thickens. Add sour cream and tomato paste alternately, stirring constantly. Simmer, do not boil. Saute beef, onions, mushrooms. Add to sauce. Simmer gently 20 minutes. Serve over cooked noodles. Serves 6.

Wyoming

REPRESENTATIVE ALAN K. SIMPSON, R.

Congressman Simpson writes, ". . . I am pleased to send on a special recipe of an oatmeal-molasses breakfast bread. It doesn't exactly rise right out of the pan but it is a hell of a good morsel! The basic recipe I obtained from an old friend in Cody, Wyoming years ago and then I added little supplements to it. I recall the days when I actually had time to bake bread — I fear those are 'gone forever' at least at the present time. . . ."
Note for runners and joggers: As any runner (we've noticed a few racing up Capitol Hill) will tell you, it's good for mind as well as body. Well any cook will tell you, so is baking bread! Prepare to see a bit of flour dusting the sleeves of our more athletic solons' sweatsuits in the future.

Oatmeal Bread

1½ cups boiling water
½ cup milk (scalded)
2 cups uncooked rolled oats
½ tsp. salt
1 tbs. butter
½ cup molasses
1 package yeast dissolved in
   ½ cup lukewarm water
1 egg, beaten
5 cups flour
3 tbs. sugar
1 cup raisins

REPRESENTATIVE ALAN K. SIMPSON, R.

Add boiling water and scalded milk to oats; stir in salt, butter and molasses. Let stand until lukewarm. Dissolve yeast in the ½ cup of lukewarm water. Add yeast mixture and beaten egg to oats mixture. Beat in flour gradually and knead dough until smooth and elastic. Let rise until double in bulk; punch down and let rise again until not quite double in bulk. Divide dough in 2 parts; mold into loaves; place in well greased loaf pans. Brush tops of loaves with melted fat, let rise. Bake for 1 hour; at 400 degrees for 10 minutes, and at 350 degrees for the remaining time.

REPRESENTATIVE GERALD B. SOLOMON, R.

"Grilling by New York Congressman" is a phase that could have more than one interpretation. But this particular grilling by this particular Congressman can just have pleasant associations. Three answers only are possible: "medium," "rare" or "well done."

Bar-B-Qued Spareribs

Sauce
¼ cup unsulfered molasses
1 tsp. chili powder
¼ cup vinegar
½ cup Worcestershire sauce
1 cup ketchup
½ tsp. Tobasco sauce
1 cup water

Mix all ingredients together in a small bowl. Set aside.

3 pounds of spareribs
1 lemon thinly sliced
1 onion thinly sliced

Put spareribs meatside up in a shallow baking dish. Lay lemon and onion slices on top. Sprinkle with salt. Bake at 350 degrees for 30 minutes. Remove spareribs from oven and baste with sauce. Place on barbecue grill and cook for one hour.

REPRESENTATIVE FLOYD SPENCE, R.

There must be times in a busy Congressional schedule when even the work hermit conjures up happy fantasies. These hermit cookies are quite real, but they, too, are a happy alternative to legislative labors.

Hermit Cookies
(Spicy Raisin Cookies)

2 cups brown sugar
1 cup of butter
2 eggs
1 cup of buttermilk
1 large teaspoon of baking soda
1 pound of raisins
1 cup of nuts
½ teaspoon of cinnamon
½ teaspoon of nutmeg
½ teaspoon of cloves
3 cups of flour (batter should be very stiff, a little more
   flour may need to be added)

Add all the ingredients together except the buttermilk and the baking soda. Mix the buttermilk and the baking soda together and add them to the other ingredients. Drop by a teaspoon onto a greased cookie sheet. Bake at 375 degrees until brown, about 12-15 minutes.

REPRESENTATIVE BOB STUMP, D.

Not your typical backyard barbecue, neither is this a dinner to whip up ahead of time, freeze and pop into the oven at the last minute. As a matter of fact the dimensions of some backyards may be smaller than those specified here for the barbecue pit. But if yours is not and if you just happen to have two hundred people coming for dinner, thanks to Congressman Stump's recipe your troubles are over.

Stump Farms Pit Barbecue

Pre-heat pit oven:

Dig a hole four feet wide, four feet deep and six feet long. Gather enough wood (preferably mesquite or any other hardwood) to fill the hole. Light fire approximately 24 hours prior to use. After the fire has burned for approximately 24 hours one should have about 2 to 3 feet of hot coals.

Meat Preparation:

Take 10, 10 pound chunks of boneless chuck or any type of boneless meat. Season with Morton Sugar Cure by rubbing liberally onto meat, shake off excess. If desired, sprinkle with garlic powder. Wrap each chunk in plain butcher paper and place in a WET burlap sack (available at any feed store). Tie tightly with wire. Have all sacks ready before placing any in the pit oven.

Barbecue:

Place all wet burlap meat packages directly on top of coals. Cover with a piece of tin, leaving room for 2 - 3 feet of dirt which is then placed on top of the tin. Make sure that no smoke escapes. Smoke indicates ventilation and fire will occur. BAKE for 24 hours. Serves 200. Dig up and serve with pinto beans, biscuits, and corn on the cob.

SENATOR ROBERT TAFT JR., R.

Lobster may not be native to Ohio, but political figures named Taft most certainly are. Senator Robert Taft Jr. favors a lobster bisque that can be whipped up in less time than it takes for a Senate roll call.

Ohio Lobster Bisque

2 chicken bouillon cubes
2 cups of boiling water
Salt, to taste
Pepper, to taste
Parsley
1 fresh lobster (cooked), 1½ to 2 pounds or 2 frozen
   lobster tails
1 pint of cream

When the lobster meat is tender, remove it from the shell. Cut it into small, bite size chunks. Add the meat to the chicken base, along with the cream, parsley, salt and pepper. Simmer for ten minutes. This will serve 4 people.

REPRESENTATIVE ROY A. TAYLOR, D.

Three of Representative Taylor's favorite recipes add up to a meal likely to fulfill the demands of one's Department of the Interior. All three need to be prepared some time before serving. Meeting departmental needs, after all, cannot be done instantaneously.

Five-Hour Stew

2 lbs. of stew meat
12 white onions
1 cup chopped celery
2 potatoes, cut into eighths
6 carrots, cut into six-inch pieces
1 slice of bread
2 (8 ounce) cans of tomato sauce
1 cup of water
1½ tsp. salt
Combine all of the ingredients in a casserole.
Cook in a 250 degree oven for five hours.

REPRESENTATIVE ROY A. TAYLOR, D.

Slaw

1 large head of cabbage, shredded
1 small onion, chopped
7/8 cup sugar

Put into a bowl. Let stand and prepare the following:

1 cup of vinegar
⅔ cup of cooking oil
2 tablespoons of sugar
2 teaspoons of prepared mustard
2 teaspoons of salt
2 teaspoons of celery seed

Boil the above ingredients, and pour over the cabbage. Let stand overnight or at least eight hours.

Easy Chocolate Squares

1 cup brown sugar
1 cup (2 sticks) margarine
1 cup chopped pecans
1 teaspoon vanilla
1 large Hershey bar
½ cup chocolate chips
Graham crackers

In a rather large pan, 12½ or 13, x 8½ or 9 inches, put whole graham crackers side by side, to cover the whole bottom of the pan.

Cook the sugar and the margarine about five minutes, stirring constantly. Remove from the heat and add nuts and vanilla. Pour this over the crackers. Bake at 375 degrees for 8-10 minutes. Cool. Add the melted Hershey bar and the chocolate chips. (Melt the chocolate over hot water, but do not let the water boil.) When the chocolate topping is set, cut into squares.

Note: The first part has to be cool in order for the chocolate topping to set without taking a long time.

SENATOR STROM THURMOND, R.

Politicians have always known the value of a well-timed smile. So, too, we learn from this recipe do those who cook for them. Senator Thurmond held the Senate floor for a record making twenty-four hours and eighteen minutes in August of 1957. It is unknown whether or not the lure of Crab Cakes brought the filibuster to a premature conclusion.

Crab Cakes

1 pound crab claw meat
2 eggs
2 tablespoons mayonnaise
1 tablespoon Kraft's horse-radish mustard
¼ teaspoon salt
1/8 teaspoon pepper
A dash of Tabasco sauce
1 tablespoon chopped parsley

Combine all of the above ingredients, including the unbeaten eggs, and mix lightly together. Form the mixture into size of cake or croquette. Do not pack firmly, but allow the mixture to be light and spongy. Roll out a package of crackers into fine crumbs. (Do not use prepared cracker crumbs). Then, pat the crumbs lightly on the crab cake and fry in deep fat just until golden brown. Remove the hot fat as soon as the croquette is golden brown. Drain on absorbent paper and serve hot with a smile!

REPRESENTATIVE LIONEL VAN DEERLIN, D.

Pan American relations can only benefit from recipes like Mrs. Van Deerlin's south of the border specialty. In a post script to the recipe Representative Van Deerlin has penned, "It should be washed down with *cerveza* (Mexican beer)!"

Tamale Casserole

1½ cups yellow cornmeal
2 tablespoons of chili powder
1 tablespoon of salt
1 cup of salad oil
Mix these ingredients together and add:
1 number 2½ can of tomatoes, chopped
1 number 1 can of cream style corn
1 number 1 can pitted black olives
2 cups (or more) cubed left-over beef, chicken or pork

Cook all of these ingredients over a low heat until the mixture thickens. Place in a covered casserole dish and bake at 350 degrees for 45 minutes.

SENATOR LOWELL P. WEICKER JR., R.

In Senator Weicker's own words this recipe "is a regional special and a family favorite." Accompanying it was a smiling eight by ten glossy photograph of the Senator who had, perhaps, just introduced a bill to committee or sampled the pudding.

Indian Pudding

½ cup of yellow corn meal
3 cups of milk
½ cup of dark molasses
⅓ stick of butter
2 tsp. of ginger
⅓ tsp. salt

Mix all of the above ingredients together, and cook in a saucepan on top of the stove, stirring until the mixture becomes thick. Put in a baking dish, and bake in a 250 degree oven for about 45 minutes.

REPRESENTATIVE RICHARD C. WHITE, D.

Both recipes from Texas show that neither handwriting nor charm has become outmoded in that state. Kathleen (Mrs. Richard C.) White wrote out her recipe and sent along its history. "I grew up in New Orleans, where oysters abound, therefore, I chose a recipe which has a southern origin and is made of oysters!"

Fried Oyster "Po-Boy"

1 jar fresh frying oysters or 2 dozen small oysters
1 bowl cornflower (about 2 cups)
salt
2, one foot long French bread loaves (ready to serve)
1 large dill pickle
3 inches of Wesson oil in a heavy pot or deep fryer
1 lemon cut in half

Drain the oysters in a colander for 3 to 5 minutes. Roll each oyster in cornflower and shake off excess. Lay the coated oysters on a cookie sheet covered with waxed paper, and refrigerate for 45 minutes. Heat oil for frying. When it is hot enough, drop the oysters in one at a time, carefully, and not too many in the pot. (Oil must be sizzling hot.) Fry the oysters until they float and are medium brown. Scoop out, drain on paper towels, and salt. Do another batch until they are all fried, drained and salted.

Cut each loaf of bread in half, and slice open the halves. Spread liberally with butter, and place on a cookie sheet. Slide the bread under the broiler only until the butter melts and the edges of the bread have slightly browned.

Slice the pickle into thin, round chips. Place the oysters in one layer on the bread. Top with a few drops of lemon juice and a couple of pickle chips.

Makes four sandwiches. Serve warm.

REPRESENTATIVE G. WILLIAM WHITEHURST, R.

"**S**ince crabmeat is a specialty in the area surrounding Hampton Roads and Chesapeake Bay," writes Representative Whitehurst, "these recipes are particularly appropriate for me to submit." Should there be a tie vote on which of Janie Whitehurst's recipes to serve, a compromise can be reached by using the crabmeat to stuff the chicken.

Crabmeat Casserole

1 quart lump crabmeat

Marinate overnight, tightly covered in the refrigerator with:

1 small grated onion
1 tbs. lemon juice
1 tsp. Tabasco
1 tbs. rosemary

The next day, blend with:

1 package Brownberry seasoned bread cubes which have been mixed with 8 tbs. melted butter.

Mix in enough mayonnaise to moisten the mixture. Bake at 350 degrees for 30 minutes. This serves 6 to 8 people.

Also, this may be used as a stuffing for:

Chicken Chesapeake

6 broiler-fryer halves
Melted butter

Place the chicken on a large baking sheet, with the skin side up. Brush with melted butter, and salt and pepper lightly. Bake for thirty minutes at 350 degrees. Turn over, brush with melted butter again, and fill the hollow generously with the crab mixture. Return the chicken to the oven, and bake an additional 30 minutes at 350 degrees.

SENATOR HARRISON A. WILLIAMS JR., D.

Happiness is different things to different people. For a hostess it's having a dish that can be prepared a day ahead of time. For Senator Williams it is sometimes coming home from a day's hot debate to this cool seafood mousse.

Senator Harrison Williams' Seafood Mousse

1 cup mayonnaise
1 small onion, chopped
¾ cup of celery, chopped fine
10 to 14 ounces of cooked shrimp or crabmeat
½ teaspoon salt
1 can tomato soup
2 small packages cream cheese
1½ tbs. gelatin (1 Knox Package = 1 tbs.)
½ cup cold water (dissolve gelatin in cold water)

Bring undiluted soup to boil, add gelatin and cool. Blend mayonnaise, onion, shrimp, salt, cream cheese until smooth. Add soup and celery and pour mixture into mold. Refrigerate overnight.

REPRESENTATIVE LARRY WINN JR., R.

In the Winn family this recipe has very special associations. It is one, according to Representative Winn, "which is a favorite of mine and Mrs. Winn traditionally makes on election night for the family, before joining our supporters for the returns." Needless to say, it's a winner.

Plaza III Steak Soup

1 pound chopped round steak
½ pound of oleo
1 cup of flour
½ gallon of water
Fresh ground pepper to taste
Omit salt
1 large carrot, diced
1 medium onion, diced
1 stalk of celery, diced
1 package of frozen mixed vegetables
½ number 303 can of tomatoes
4 tablespoons of beef base granules

Make a roux: A roux is a mixture of flour and fat, combined in varying proportions, and heated slowly over a very low heat for anywhere from 10 to 15 minutes to 15 hours.

Brown the oleo, stir in the flour, and gradually add 2 cups of the water. Stir until smooth. Add all of the other ingredients except the ground round steak. Set aside in another pan. Saute the ground round steak in two tablespoons of oleo until it is browned. Drain off the grease. Add the meat to the first mixture and simmer, stirring occasionally for 1½ hours, or until the vegetables are tender. If the soup needs thickening, add more roux. This may be frozen for later use, and will make one gallon of Steak Soup.

INDEX

Note: See also Index by State, page 123
Index by Congressmen, page 120

A

C

INDEX BY CONGRESSMAN

SENATORS

REPRESENTATIVES

* ex officio members of Congress

** deceased

INDEX BY STATE